YOU KNO...
A DIY ADDIC...

GW00818501

Ed Cobham

SUMMERSDALE

Summersdale Publishers Ltd
46 West Street
Chichester
PO19 1RP
UK

www.summersdale.com

ISBN 1 84024 268 X

Printed and bound in Great Britain

Cartoons by Kate Taylor

YOU KNOW YOU'RE A DIY ADDICT WHEN . . .

You have started to build your own mausoleum and at the rate you're going, you'll need it quite soon.

YOU KNOW YOU'RE A DIY ADDICT WHEN . . .

You dump your lover…at the local amenity tip. That flat pack girlfriend of yours is only really fit for the heap.

YOU KNOW YOU'RE A DIY ADDICT WHEN . . .

YOU KNOW YOU'RE A DIY ADDICT WHEN . . .

You watch a few medical documentaries and decide that you are now ready to attempt your own vasectomy. Your next job will be to fix your leaky pipe.

YOU KNOW YOU'RE A DIY ADDICT WHEN . . .

Your greatest chat up line is can is: 'Fancy a screw? Would you prefer *Phillips* or *Flat Head?*'

YOU KNOW YOU'RE A DIY ADDICT WHEN . . .

Your friends suggest you get a life…so you try and build one instead.

Your wife wishes you could cook as well as you rivet but your only recipe is a recipe for disaster.

9

YOU KNOW YOU'RE A DIY ADDICT WHEN . . .

Your newborn baby leaves home in protest…because the cot you built her collapsed.

YOU KNOW YOU'RE A DIY ADDICT WHEN . . .

You build friendships easily…with lifesize matchstick men.

11

YOU KNOW YOU'RE A DIY ADDICT WHEN . . .

You don't count sheep, you count tools.

YOU KNOW YOU'RE A DIY ADDICT WHEN . . .

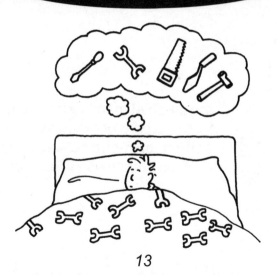

YOU KNOW YOU'RE A DIY ADDICT WHEN . . .

You laugh at friends who spend money on so-called professionals. You don't realise that they're having the last laugh as your house falls down.

14

YOU KNOW YOU'RE A DIY ADDICT WHEN . . .

You've managed to rebuild your own fingers after cutting them off by mistake.

YOU KNOW YOU'RE A DIY ADDICT WHEN . . .

You save on dentistry bills by grouting your teeth when you need a filling.

YOU KNOW YOU'RE A DIY ADDICT WHEN . . .

You are arrested for vandalising the *Lloyds Building*. You were only trying to help…you thought it was scaffolding.

Your doorbell ringer sounds suspiciously like '*If I had a hammer...*'. Or at least it would be if your door hadn't fallen off.

YOU KNOW YOU'RE A DIY ADDICT WHEN . . .

Your mobile phone ringer is Craig Phillips' delightful Christmas single.

YOU KNOW YOU'RE A DIY ADDICT WHEN . . .

You learnt to prime wood before you could talk.

YOU KNOW YOU'RE A DIY ADDICT WHEN . . .

Your partner leaves you citing Carol Smillie in the divorce.

You christen your newborn baby *Bob the Builder*. That's quite a name for a girl.

YOU KNOW YOU'RE A DIY ADDICT WHEN . . .

You learnt to push a wheelbarrow before you could walk.

You've replaced photos of your family with signed photos of Linda Barker and Laurence Llewellyn Bowen.

YOU KNOW YOU'RE A DIY ADDICT WHEN . . .

Your idea of a romantic evening is reciting chapters from a DIY manual to your lover.

In the throes of passion you take careful measurements and make sure you've the right size attachment for the hole before insertion.

YOU KNOW YOU'RE A DIY ADDICT WHEN . . .

You are on first name terms with all the nurses in your local A&E department.

YOU KNOW YOU'RE A DIY ADDICT WHEN . . .

Your parents haven't spoken to you in ages…because the phone you installed for them doesn't actually work.

You give yourself a double-barrelled name, grow a mane of hair and start wearing frilly shirts.

YOU KNOW YOU'RE A DIY ADDICT WHEN . . .

You were admitted to a mental institution when you mislaid your *Black and Decker WorkBench* but, thankfully, you were able to dig a tunnel to freedom.

You can rout faster than you can write.

YOU KNOW YOU'RE A DIY ADDICT WHEN . . .

Your first words were…*pass the hammer, please.*

YOU KNOW YOU'RE
A DIY ADDICT WHEN . . .

You build a chastity belt for your wife to wear when you are absent on a DIY courses. You can't understand how she's pregnant upon your return.

YOU KNOW YOU'RE A DIY ADDICT WHEN . . .

You are arrested for holding up a bank...with some sticky-backed plastic and a staple gun.

You've always been a keen reader…you can't understand why schools don't teach the works of Handy Andy instead of Thomas Hardy.

YOU KNOW YOU'RE A DIY ADDICT WHEN . . .

You give your lover a massage using a *Black and Decker* sander but have to apologise that you've only got the rough stuff left, but convince her it'll be good for her bad circulation.

Your friends think you're an alcoholic...
because you're obsessed with your
spirit level.

YOU KNOW YOU'RE A DIY ADDICT WHEN . . .

Your wife complains about your extension… she was hoping you'd get it up in less than six months.

YOU KNOW YOU'RE A DIY ADDICT WHEN . . .

The first thing you do in the morning is *do-it-yourself* . . . at least *that's* never fallen down.

Your builder's arse gives such good cleavage that you win a modelling contract with a prestigious bra company.

Everyone thinks you're prematurely grey…but actually it's just paint. (And to set the record straight, it's Magnolia not Grey.)

YOU KNOW YOU'RE A DIY ADDICT WHEN . . .

Your friends admire the way you knocked your living room into your dining room...what they don't realise is that you were banging a picture hook in a little too vigorously.

YOU KNOW YOU'RE A DIY ADDICT WHEN . . .

Your girlfriend leaves you because you stubbornly refuse to let a professional check out your stopcock. Having both tried, neither of you seem to be able to turn it on.

YOU KNOW YOU'RE A DIY ADDICT WHEN . . .

A typical evening alone is spent fiddling with your nuts…and bolts.

Your new lover asks you to do
something kinky with your nails...but
crucifixion wasn't what she expected.

Your girlfriend requests that you fill her crack…and is disappointed when you delve into your trousers for a tube of… *PolyFilla.*

YOU KNOW YOU'RE A DIY ADDICT WHEN . . .

When people complain that your shelves are wonky, you give them wonky glasses to rectify matters rather than admit fault.

YOU KNOW YOU'RE A DIY ADDICT WHEN . . .

The alphabet only seems to consist of three letters…DIY.

You build a rabbit hutch…even though you don't own any rabbits.

You try to repair the hole in your marriage with sealant.

**YOU KNOW YOU'RE
A DIY ADDICT WHEN . . .**

Your living room has had more make-overs than Posh and Becks.

YOU KNOW YOU'RE A DIY ADDICT WHEN . . .

Your idea of getting steamy…is the *Earlex Super Steamer Kit* for £32.99.

57

YOU KNOW YOU'RE
A DIY ADDICT WHEN . . .

Your wife hits menopause and you treat her cranky bits with WD40.

You think cable TV is a station network devoted to power leads.

YOU KNOW YOU'RE
A DIY ADDICT WHEN . . .

You are saving up for a cord extension
in order to give your wife that extra bit
of length she deserves.

YOU KNOW YOU'RE A DIY ADDICT WHEN . . .

You are always telling people the importance of etiquette: never forget your *B&Qs*.

You have rigged up CCTV in the garden shed you built...so you can watch your tools from the comfort of your living room.

You know *who* Nick Knowles is, but you don't know *why* he is.

YOU KNOW YOU'RE A DIY ADDICT WHEN . . .

Your wife calls you one of her *Big Strong Boys*. You don't realise that she'd prefer *Jake* or *Gavin* any day.

YOU KNOW YOU'RE A DIY ADDICT WHEN . . .

Father Christmas sues you for the damage done when falling down your architecturally unsound chimney.

YOU KNOW YOU'RE A DIY ADDICT WHEN . . .

After you report pains in your stomach, your GP suggests that you might need help with your waterworks and is perplexed when you rush out and buy some new copper piping.

YOU KNOW YOU'RE A DIY ADDICT WHEN . . .

Your preferred career (other than DIY expert) is that of *Halal* butcher...well, you're great at bleeding a radiator: why should a cow be any different?

Your girlfriend takes offence when you offer to strim her bikini line.

Your teenage daughter asks for a makeover for her birthday and disappointed when you get her *primed* and *pebbledashed*.

Your favourite snack is *cornice* pasties.

Your favourite meal is fish and
woodchips.

**YOU KNOW YOU'RE
A DIY ADDICT WHEN . . .**

You don't judge people by their colour
or screed.

YOU KNOW YOU'RE A DIY ADDICT WHEN . . .

You were disappointed at your stag night when your mates provided you with a female stripper. What's wrong with the *Black and Decker* hand-held one?

Your favourite theme at the local night-club would be *Tongue and Groove*.

Your wife leaves you for someone who
shows more emulsion.

You are very understanding when your son complains of a bad case of wet rot in his hardwood.

YOU KNOW YOU'RE A DIY ADDICT WHEN . . .

Your adolescent daughter wants her bedroom redecorated and you aptly suggest *Period Style*.

You hold your wedding list at *Homebase*. Actually, you hold your wedding there too. Marching your bride up the *Power Tools* aisle was a defining moment for you.

YOU KNOW YOU'RE
A DIY ADDICT WHEN . . .

HOMEBASE
Wedding
List
Cement mixer
Work bench
Screwdrivers
Sander
Spirit level
Tool Box
Ladders

YOU KNOW YOU'RE
A DIY ADDICT WHEN . . .

You insist that the family's pet hamster
exercises on a *colour wheel*.

You never leave the house without an undercoat…after all, it's important to protect your fixtures and fittings.

The only paper you read is the wallpaper.

YOU KNOW YOU'RE A DIY ADDICT WHEN . . .

**YOU KNOW YOU'RE
A DIY ADDICT WHEN . . .**

You build a bridge to your lover's heart but it collapses under the strain of your *tool*.

YOU KNOW YOU'RE A DIY ADDICT WHEN . . .

On Valentine's Day you plan to ply your wife with all sorts of goodies, but get side tracked and ply her...literally with pliers. Ouch.

YOU KNOW YOU'RE
A DIY ADDICT WHEN . . .

The ladies think you are such a sensitive soul, as you always carry paint cards with you in order to ascertain their eye colour. They don't realise until it's too late that you're just a sad git.

YOU KNOW YOU'RE A DIY ADDICT WHEN . . .

You know your *warp* from your *weft*.

YOU KNOW YOU'RE A DIY ADDICT WHEN . . .

You apply for augmentation surgery to achieve a proper *builder's bum*. The surgeon turns you away, thinking you've already been done.

YOU KNOW YOU'RE A DIY ADDICT WHEN . . .

You could wire a plug blindfolded. In fact, you do. You kinky bugger.

YOU KNOW YOU'RE A DIY ADDICT WHEN . . .

You call the new family pet *Dimmock*... well, it's a great dog's name.

YOU KNOW YOU'RE
A DIY ADDICT WHEN . . .

Your wife wants breast implants and you offer to spare her the expense seeing as you can get a trade discount on sandbags.

You build a *Trojan Horse* for your Classics-loving son, but he rejects it having been warned against *geeks bearing gifts*.

YOU KNOW YOU'RE A DIY ADDICT WHEN . . .

You fantasise about the woman in the hardware store. She has promised to show you her bits one day…and you're particularly keen on her drill bits.

**YOU KNOW YOU'RE
A DIY ADDICT WHEN . . .**

You buy your partner a *dado* when she requests something interesting for the bedroom. She suggests you get your ears syringed.

The Department of Trade and Industry have got your number…but are far too scared to ring it for fear of what they might learn.

**YOU KNOW YOU'RE
A DIY ADDICT WHEN . . .**

You are used in an advertising
campaign on how *not* to do-it-yourself.
You are still flattered.

You have tattooed your own disclaimer on your arm just in case…trouble is, no-one can actually read it for all the blood and loose flesh.

Your favourite band would have to be... *The Carpenters* (groan).

YOU KNOW YOU'RE A DIY ADDICT WHEN . . .

You buy your 8-year-old niece a mitre saw for her birthday, not the jigsaw she is hankering after.

YOU KNOW YOU'RE A DIY ADDICT WHEN . . .

Given the choice between an Amsterdam w*nking booth and your flat-pack garden shed, you'd go for the latter every time.

YOU KNOW YOU'RE A DIY ADDICT WHEN . . .

YOU KNOW YOU'RE
A DIY ADDICT WHEN . . .

You learnt to drive a *JCB digger* before you could even ride a bike.

YOU KNOW YOU'RE A DIY ADDICT WHEN . . .

You installed your own gas central heating, which might explain why your house has exploded.

Sex is spelt MDF.

110

Your partner is very proud of your impressive erection...and your penis for that matter.

YOU KNOW YOU'RE A DIY ADDICT WHEN . . .

Your favourite cocktail would have to be a *long hard screw* **in** *the wall*.

112

YOU KNOW YOU'RE A DIY ADDICT WHEN . . .

The paddling pool you dig for your kids becomes an international concern, as your little ones resurface on the Sydney coastline 24 hours later.

When you run out of nappies for your toddler, you just slosh some damp proofing on her.

YOU KNOW YOU'RE A DIY ADDICT WHEN . . .

You change your name by deed poll to *Stanley Knife*.

You insist that your wife changes her
name to *Robert Dyas*.

You take your family for picnics at the local garden centre.

**YOU KNOW YOU'RE
A DIY ADDICT WHEN . . .**

Your idea of looking festive is painting
yourself in *Hammerite*.

YOU KNOW YOU'RE A DIY ADDICT WHEN . . .

As a DIY enthusiast, there's nothing you can't fix…except for your mental state as an obsessive-compulsive.

YOU KNOW YOU'RE
A DIY ADDICT WHEN . . .

Your partner is keen on getting her
nipples pierced. At last, your very own
set of tungsten tips to play with…

YOU KNOW YOU'RE A DIY ADDICT WHEN . . .

You try to rebuild your cat after it's squashed by your collapsing shelves.

123

LOUISE McKAY

101 USES FOR A FOOTBALL

summersdale humour

ED COBHAM

YOU KNOW YOU'RE A FOOTBALL FANATIC WHEN . . .

summersdale humour

EMMA BURGESS

101 USES FOR THE ROYAL FAMILY

summersdale humour

emma burgess

GIRL POWER - the rules

summersdale humour

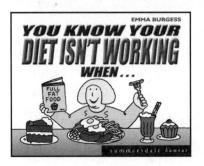

EMMA BURGESS

YOU KNOW YOUR
DIET ISN'T WORKING
WHEN . . .

FULL FAT FOOD

summersdale *humour*

EMMA BURGESS

YOU KNOW YOU'RE A
MANEATER
WHEN . . .

summersdale *humour*

NICK FERRIS

REVENGE

101 THINGS TO DO
WHEN YOU'VE
BEEN DUMPED

DANGER
EXPLOSIVE

summersdale *humour*

YOU KNOW YOU'RE A
COMPUTER NERD
WHEN . . .

SUMMERSDALE

**For the latest humour books
from Summersdale, check out**

www.summersdale.com